FLIGHTS & MANEUVERS

ZOOM

TO FLY RAPIDLY STRAIGHT UPWARDS.

BANK

TO TURN THE AIRPLANE IN A CIRCLE WITH THE WINGS AT AN ANGLE TO THE GROUND.

IRELAND

WALES

— — — — Amelia Earhart's Record Flights
FRIENDSHIP Flight

GLIDE

TO FLY DOWNWARD WITHOUT THE MOTOR OF THE AIRPLANE RUNNING.

DIVE

TO FLY DOWNWARD STEEPLY AND RAPIDLY WITH OR WITHOUT THE MOTOR RUNNING.

Robert Quackenbush

CLEAR THE COW PASTURE, I'M COMING IN FOR A LANDING!

A Story of Amelia Earhart

SIMON AND SCHUSTER BOOKS FOR YOUNG READERS

Published by Simon & Schuster Inc., New York

Simon and Schuster Books for Young Readers
Simon & Schuster Building
Rockefeller Center
1230 Avenue of the Americas
New York, New York 10020

SIMON AND SCHUSTER BOOKS FOR YOUNG READERS
is a trademark of Simon & Schuster Inc.

Manufactured in the United States of America

10 9 8 7 6 5 4 3 2 1
10 9 8 7 6 5 4 3 2 1 pbk.

Library of Congress Cataloging-in-Publication Data

Quackenbush, Robert M.
   Clear the cow pasture, I'm coming in for a landing! : a
story of Amelia Earhart / by Robert Quackenbush.
      p.   cm.
   SUMMARY: A biography of the courageous aviatrix
who became the first woman to fly across the Atlantic.
   l. Earhart, Amelia, 1897-1937—Juvenile literature. 2. Air
pilots—United States—Biography—Juvenile literature.
[l. Earhart, Amelia, 1897-1937. 2. Air pilots.]   I. Title.
TL540.E3Q33   1990
629.13'092—dc20
[B]   [92]   89-6164   CIP   AC
ISBN 0-671-68548-1
ISBN 0-671-69218-6 pbk.

For Piet and Margie

There once was a girl named Amelia Earhart, who was born on July 24, 1897 in Atchison, Kansas. Amelia had a sister named Muriel, who was three years younger. When the girls were little, they wouldn't play like other little girls in the neighborhood. They put on comfortable outfits called bloomers so they could run around and play as roughly as the boys did. They climbed trees, played baseball, fished, jumped fences, and walked on stilts. In those days adults frowned on little girls who wore bloomers instead of dresses and played like boys. But the sisters' parents heartily approved. After all, their mother had been the first woman to climb to the top of Pike's Peak in Colorado. "Dear Dad," Amelia wrote one Christmas, "Muriel and I would like footballs this year, please. We need them especially as we have plenty of baseballs, bats, etc. ..."

Amelia acquired an adventurous spirit from her mother and a love of travel and a vivid imagination from her father. Her father was a lawyer for the railroads and often took the family with him on business trips. He told Amelia and Muriel exciting stories that ran on and on for weeks. He played word games with them and they tried to trip him up with hard words from the dictionary. He responded with bewildering words like one in a letter he wrote to Amelia that began "Dear parallele-pipedon." But there was something about him that made the family very unhappy. Mr. Earhart was often drunk. Because of his drinking, he lost several jobs and had to keep moving the family to find new work. They moved to Des Moines, Iowa; St. Paul, Minnesota; and Springfield, Missouri. Amelia finished her secondary education in Chicago, in 1916, after attending six high schools because of the moves. Even so, she was not bitter toward her father, and she always had sympathy for people with drinking problems.

After finishing high school, Amelia went away to college in Pennsylvania. During a break at Christmas, she visited Muriel, who was attending college in Toronto, Canada. It was 1917 and World War I was raging in Europe. While in Toronto, Amelia saw four young men hobbling down the street. They were survivors of the war and each of them had only one leg. Seeing this, Amelia wanted to do something for the war effort. She quit school and became a nurse's aide at Toronto's Spadina Military Hospital. Some of the patients she attended were military pilots. She was fascinated by the stories they told about their aerial dogfights over the battlefields of Europe. She wanted to know more about flying. In her spare time she went to local fairs to see ace pilots perform stunts. Then she took a course in automobile engine mechanics to learn how engines worked.

13

In 1919, World War I ended. Amelia decided to return to college. She went to New York to study medicine at Columbia University. At the end of her first year, she moved to Los Angeles, where her parents and Muriel were living. Her plan was to finish her medical training there, specializing in research. But she had not forgotten about airplanes. Her father took her to an air show and bought her a ticket for a ten-minute ride in an airplane. After that first flight, Amelia knew that flying was the *only* thing she wanted to do. How could she afford lessons? she wondered. They cost a thousand dollars in 1920, and her father could not afford them. She made up her mind to quit school and find work to pay for the lessons herself. She took a job as a file clerk at the telephone company.

15

Amelia's family seldom saw her after the flying lessons began. She worked at her job all week and spent weekends at the airport. Her flying instructor was Neta Snook, who was the first female graduate of the Curtis School of Aviation. In those pioneer days of aviation, flying was usually reserved for men. Amelia and Neta stood out at the flying field. But Amelia would not let that stand in her way. Just as she had done as a child to keep up with the boys in the neighborhood, now she dressed like the men at the airport. She cropped her hair short and wore a rough leather flight jacket, goggles, and comfortable slacks. Soon she was accepted by the other pilots. Amelia learned to fly on a course and how to land. She learned the three s's of aviation—slips, stalls, and spins.

17

Amelia was eager for more flying time so she could earn a license. She took on extra work to pay for more lessons, including driving a truck for a sand-and-gravel company. At last she was ready for a solo flight. She flew up to 5,000 feet (1,500 m), played around a little in the clouds, and came back. All went well except for a poor landing. She needed a lot more practice. She kept on with her lessons. Finally, two years later, in the summer of 1922, she earned her pilot's license. She was one of a dozen licensed women flyers in the world. For a birthday surprise her mother and sister helped her buy a secondhand plane. It was a bright yellow biplane called a Kinner Canary. Now Amelia could fly whenever she wanted.

In her Kinner Canary, Amelia practiced until she could fly well in rain, sunshine, and snow. Then she entered an air show. She soared at 14,000 feet (4,200 m)—almost 3 miles. Suddenly, the engine quit and the plane went into a dive. Amelia calmly shut off the fuel switches so that electric sparks would not set the fuel on fire. Steadily, she pulled the control stick back until she eased the airplane out of the dive. Then she made a safe landing at the airfield. She was greeted by her relieved family and a crowd of cheering spectators. Her flight created a new world record for altitude reached by a pilot. Encouraged by this success, Amelia tried to find work in aviation. Unfortunately, there was none. She was forced to sell her plane and give up flying for a while. For several years after that, Amelia drifted back and forth between college classes and jobs. She watched from the sidelines while aviators tested their planes on long-distance flights. The most exciting flight was made by Charles Lindberg on May 21, 1927. He became the first person to fly solo across the Atlantic Ocean.

Spirit of St. Louis

Charles Lindberg

Lindberg flew from New York to Paris—a distance of 3,610 miles (5,776 km)—in 33 hours and 30 minutes. After the event, Mrs. Frederick Guest, a flying enthusiast from London, England, decided a woman should cross the Atlantic, too. She bought a big seaplane and named it the *Friendship*. The name symbolized the goodwill that existed between the United States and Great Britain. Mrs. Guest hired two Americans—Captain Hilton Railey, head of a public relations firm, and George Palmer Putnam, a book publisher—to find the right woman for the flight. Railey and Putnam knew about a lady flyer who was working in Boston as a social worker. She was teaching English and playing games with immigrant children at settlement houses. Perhaps, said Railey and Putnam, the person they had in mind could be persuaded to leave her job. She had the same light-colored tousled hair, shyness, and all-American grin as Charles Lindberg, which should please the London backers. Her name? Amelia Earhart.

"Lady Lindy"

Amelia jumped at the chance to be the first woman to cross the Atlantic, though she was to be just a passenger on the *Friendship*. It would be a perilous undertaking. The crew would be facing the unknown as modern astronauts do when they venture into space. Already in those early days of flight, three women had died trying to make the same crossing. But Amelia was not afraid. On June 3, 1928, the *Friendship* took off from Boston and landed at Treshassy Bay, Newfoundland for refueling. On June 7 the heavily loaded plane left Newfoundland and flew eastward above the Atlantic. After a few hours in the air, the plane was flying in dense clouds and the radio went dead. The pilot, Wilmer Stultz, and the mechanic, Louis Gordon, had to rely on instruments to fly through the night. When dawn came, the clouds parted and the three pilots saw an ocean liner. They tried to signal the liner to see which way they were flying, but they received no response. They kept on flying in a direction that Stultz hoped would lead to shore, for the sea was too choppy to make a landing. With only one hour of fuel left, Stultz finally shouted "Land!" He sat the plane down in the harbor off the coast of Burry Point, Wales.

The *Friendship* made the crossing in 20 hours and 40 minutes. Amelia Earhart had become the first woman to cross the Atlantic by air. But their landing went almost unnoticed at first. Amelia waved a white towel from the cockpit. A man on shore saw her and waved, but kept on walking. Finally, a boat came out to pick up the crew. Suddenly, Amelia Earhart was a name heard 'round the world. Her picture was published in newspapers everywhere and reporters nicknamed her "Lady Lindy." When she returned to New York, she and the crew were given a ticker-tape parade down Broadway. At the same time, offers were thrust at Amelia to give lectures and demonstrations, write articles, and advertise products. She promised to write a book for George Putnam. The volume was called *20 Hours, 40 Minutes; Our Flight in the Friendship.* After the book was finished, Putnam became her manager. He made money for her by using her name to advertise products like luggage and chewing gum. Now she could buy a brand new plane of her own. In 1932, she married Putnam, with the understanding that marriage would not stand in the way of her career and love of flying.

It was difficult for Amelia Earhart to enjoy her sudden fame. She felt that there was something false about it, since she was merely a passenger in the *Friendship*. So for the next four years she set out to prove that she really was the first woman of aviation. In September 1928, she was the first woman to solo on a transcontinental round-trip. In November 1928, she set a speed record for women in Los Angeles, California. In June 1930, she set a speed record for just over 600 miles (100 km) in Detroit, Michigan. She also flew an autogiro, an aircraft that was part airplane and part helicopter, to set more records. In this odd-looking machine she climbed to a record 18,451 feet (5,535 m), or about 3½ miles, at Willow Grove, Pennsylvania, in April 1931. Then, in 1932, she made a startling announcement to the press. She was preparing to fly over the Atlantic in a plane without floats—or pontoons—in place of wheels. If she was forced to land on water, her plane would sink. True to her word, on May 20, 1932—five years to the day after Lindberg started his historic flight—Amelia began her mission. She took off from Harbor Grace, Newfoundland, in the Vega that she had bought with her earnings from book royalties and lectures.

A few hours after takeoff, Amelia faced trouble. Her altimeter failed and she could not tell how far she was above the ocean. Then flames shot out from a crack in the engine exhaust. As if this was not enough, she flew smack into a storm. Still, Amelia kept on her course. She tried to take her plane above the storm, but ice formed on the wings. This was extremely dangerous because ice adds weight to the wings and could cause an airplane to crash. Quickly, Amelia spun the Vega down toward warmer air to melt the ice. As she broke through the storm clouds, she saw she was about to hit the sea. Just in time, she managed to pull the plane into level flight above the waves. For many hours Amelia braved the treacherous elements and piloted her vibrating plane with the exhaust still flaming. Finally, she saw land. She circled and brought her Vega down in a cow pasture in Ireland. The independent girl from Kansas, who believed that women had the right to try the same things men did, had succeeded! She was the first woman to fly solo across the Atlantic. She did it in 15 hours and 18 minutes. She was also the first woman to cross the ocean *twice* by air.

31

In Europe, Amelia Earhart was entertained by royalty and she received many medals and honors for her courage in the air. When she returned to the United States the celebration continued. She was entertained at the White House and received many more medals, including the distinguished Flying Cross for outstanding achievement in aviation. But this was only the beginning for Amelia. For the next several years, she continued to set numerous flying records and to receive more awards. In August 1932, she set the women's nonstop transcontinental speed record from Los Angeles, California to Newark, New Jersey. In July 1933, she broke her own record for that same flight. In January 1935, she became the first person to fly from Hawaii to California, the first person to solo anywhere in the Pacific, and the first person to solo over both Atlantic and Pacific oceans. In April 1935, she became the first person to solo from Los Angeles, California to Mexico City, Mexico. In May 1935, she became the first person to solo from Mexico to Newark, New Jersey. In March 1937, she set a record for an east to west flight from Oakland, California, to Honolulu, Hawaii. Her record flights changed the world's opinion of women as pilots and helped to launch the aviation industry.

In 1937, Amelia Earhart set out to be the first woman to fly around the world and the first pilot to fly around the equator —a distance of 27,000 miles (43,200 km). Her plane was an all-metal Electra with two engines that she named the *Flying Laboratory*. After one failed attempt, caused by her plane crashing on the runway in Honolulu, the airplane was repaired and a new flight heading eastward began from Oakland, California on May 20, 1937. Amelia's navigator was Fred Noonan. They flew to Miami, Florida; South America; Africa; India; Burma; Indonesia; Australia; and Lae, New Guinea—a total distance of 22,000 miles (35,200 km). The two fliers now faced the most dangerous part of the flight across the Pacific. Their first stop was to be on Howland Island on a specially built runway that was ordered by President Roosevelt. It was to be a refueling stop 2,556 miles (4,090 km) from Lae. But they never arrived. Somewhere in the area of the tiny island Amelia Earhart and Fred Noonan vanished without a trace. Ships and planes were sent and millions of dollars were spent to search for them. After fifteen days the search was abandoned and the brave flyers were officially listed "lost at sea." And so, Amelia Earhart's last great flight was an unfinished achievement.

ᑯᔆᔆᔆ Epilogue ᑯᔆᔆᔆ

For many years, navigators, scientists, and reporters searched for clues to the disappearance of Amelia Earhart. Some investigators believe that she was on a spy mission for the United States and that she and Fred Noonan were captured by the enemy and executed. Others believe that the plane was lost in cloudy weather conditions, ran out of fuel, and crashed into the sea. The search still continues today. Perhaps this is because people do not want to believe that she is truly gone. She was admired by millions for her brilliant career as a pioneer in the aviation industry. She urged women not to be afraid and to be as adventurous as men. She paved the way for other remarkable women in aviation and aeronautics in the space age. These women include Jacqueline Cochran, an outstanding pilot who won many awards and prizes, and Judith Resnik and Christa McAuliffe, the brave women of the *Challenger.* All of these women have stressed to other women how important it is to take chances in their pursuit of richer and more fulfilling lives.

36

AMELIA EARHART IN HER OWN WORDS

20 Hrs. 40 Min. New York: G.P. Putnam's Sons, 1928.
The Fun of It. New York: Harcourt Brace and Company, 1937.
Last Flight. (Edited by George Palmer Putnam). New York:
Harcourt Brace and Company, 1937.

SPIRAL

TO FLY DOWNWARD IN CIRCLES LIKE THE COILS OF A SPRING.

TAIL SPIN

IN WHICH THE AIRPLANE SPINS TOWARD THE EARTH NOSE DOWN.

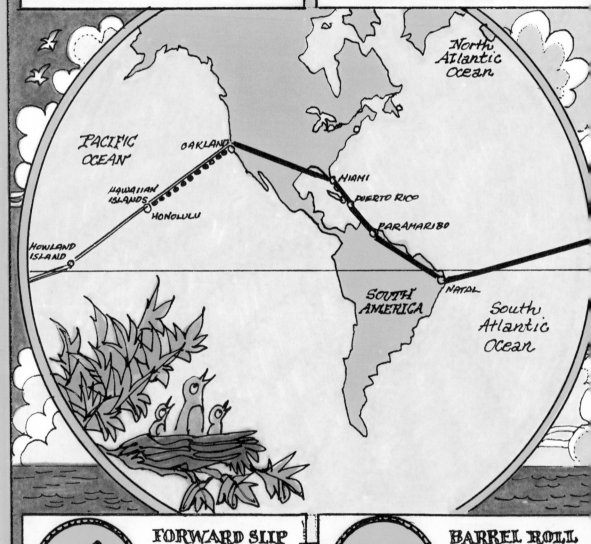

North Atlantic Ocean

PACIFIC OCEAN

OAKLAND

MIAMI

PUERTO RICO

HAWAIIAN ISLANDS

HONOLULU

PARAMARIBO

HOWLAND ISLAND

SOUTH AMERICA

NATAL

South Atlantic Ocean

FORWARD SLIP

TO FLY DOWNWARD IN A SLIGHTLY BANKED POSITION SO THAT FORWARD SPEED AND FORWARD TRAVEL ARE ABOUT EQUAL.

BARREL ROLL

A STUNT USUALLY PERFORMED BY MILITARY PILOTS TO MAKE THE AIRPLANE TURN OVER AND OVER WHILE FLYING FORWARD.